For You

Andreas Seidl

Handover of Power

Eurpean Version

Volume 10: Barter Economy

Imprint

Bibliographic information of the German National Library:
The German National Library lists this publication in the
German National Bibliography; detailed bibliographic data
are available on the Internet at http://dnb.dnb.de.

© 2022 Dipl. Pol. Theodor Andreas Seidl

Cover: Christiane Ebrecht
Translation: DeepL, Cologne
Production and publishing: BoD – Books on Demand,
Norderstedt

ISBN: 978-3-7568-0258-6

Acknowledgements

My thanks go to my family and friends who have made me who I am today. Special thanks to all those who supported me in writing this book. I would like to thank all my classmates, teachers, fellow students, lecturers, demonstrators, activists, colleagues, companies and countries with whom I have had the privilege of sharing the experiences from which all the ideas in this book have emerged. I would like to thank the staff of Books on Demand for their kind helpfulness. I thank the citizens of Seligenstadt for the harmony and solidarity in which I was able to write.

Foreword

This policy concept contains a variety of proposals for possible political reforms. It can be peacefully and democratically adapted to any current political system of any state in the world, but also to political systems in families, clubs, associations or companies. Wherever humans make or submit to rules that manage living together, the following proposals can be helpful. Readers who find the proposals so helpful that they would like to implement them together with like-minded people can contact the author. The contact form on the last page can be used for this purpose.

Faults and defects
I ask for your understanding that this volume was not professionally proofread. I could only afford professional proofreading for the summary. Spelling errors and unfortunate phrasing may therefore occur. As soon as this volume has sold enough to pay for a professional proofreading, it will be done. After that, a new edition will be published.

English version
Please understand that this volume has been translated automatically. I could only afford a professional translation for the summary. Poor wording and spelling errors may therefore occur. In case of doubt, the German version shall prevail. As soon as this volume has sold enough to pay for a professional translation, it will be done. After that, a new edition will be

published. It was more important to me that no one in the world should have an information advantage than individual translation errors in the complete work.

References
If something has been quoted directly, it is set in italics. If the headings contain footnotes, the sources for direct and indirect quotations apply in the chapter for which the heading stands. Otherwise, quotations or source references are directly at the word or at the end of the sentence or paragraph. This book contains parts of text based on the Federal Constitution of the Swiss Confederation of 18 April 1999 (as of 12 February 2017), abbreviated to BV[1] and the Constitution of the Canton of Bern of 6 June 1993 (as of 11 March 2015), abbreviated to KV[2] .

If the constitutional paragraph, or individual paragraphs thereof, are based in whole or in part on extracts from the BV or KV, this is indicated in a footnote. The references to the corresponding footnotes for constitutional paragraphs are usually found after the heading of the affected chapter and sometimes in the body of the text. Articles used in the Swiss constitutions are listed in the footnote with a number after the title of the constitutional paragraph. Example: §123 Sample title: BV Art.123, KV Art.123.

All internet sources are fully cited in the footnotes. They were last accessed on 30.09.2021. All literature sources are also listed in full in the footnotes.

All references to tasks undertaken by other ministries and described in more detail there are given in footnotes. Example: Model Ministry - 1.2.3 Model Chapter.

All footnotes are to be viewed in comparison to the respective source, so-called indirect quotations. Direct quotations are set in italics, but hardly ever occur. The source reference is intended to enable further investigation and to take copyright

---

1 This is not an official publication. Only the publication by the Swiss Federal Chancellery is authoritative. https://www.fedlex.admin.ch/eli/cc/1999/404/de On 14.12.2021

2 This is not an official publication. The Bernese Official Collection of Laws is authoritative. https://www.belex.sites.be.ch/frontend/versions/2420?locale=de#ART71 On 16.12.2021

into account.

All keywords used, based on the names of the responsible units, departments and ministries of Germany, are listed at the end of this volume in the chapter on the conversion of ministries.

Table of contents

1 Goals of the Ministry for Barter Economy

The Barter Economy represents a life of freedom and poverty in the four economic forms. The Ministry of Barter Economy ensures freedom of choice for nationals to decide for themselves what level of freedom or security they prefer in their lives. Whether citizens live temporarily or entirely in the Barter Economy, the primal nature experiences of individual citizens will be enriching for the people as a whole. Humans who desire a decelerated, natural, simple, abstemious or traditional life can become hermits or settlers in one of the three comfort zones.

Money is not necessary for survival, but it is for the entrance. There are three comfort levels to buy into. The lowest comfort level is life as it was in primeval times. Residents live here without technical goods that do not rot and cannot be found directly in the surrounding nature. The middle comfort level is a life similar to the Middle Ages, but with certain modern exceptions so that the environment is not polluted. The highest comfort level is living in caravans or in containers at the edge of the Barter Economy Zone with connections to the water, sewage, data and electricity network.

The Barter Economy, through its existence, provides a safeguard for disasters such as a pole reversal of the Earth's magnetic field, along with solar winds that cripple devices with computer chips. In the event of such a disaster, the Ministry of Barter Economy works with the Ministry of Security. Current residents then become teachers for the rest of the population on how to survive without technical devices and electricity.

2 Departments

The departments are divided into sub-departments and enumerations are usually considered as their individual units. Many tasks of some departments are completely taken over by other ministries as a service.

2.1 Central Department

Part of the Central Department is the Reception Office with the Courier and Mail Room, which directs all concerns, broadcasts and visitors to the appropriate place in the ministry.

2.1.1 Staff

The Human Resources Department is responsible for staff development and planning. For this purpose, it takes care of the recruitment of junior staff, intern and trainee programmes as well as the selection procedures for employees and special selection procedures for applicants with disabilities. For politicians and employees, the department prepares a job plan. In all its tasks, it works in voting with the personnel board.[1]

All other personnel matters are transferred to the respective ministries. The Ministry of Education is responsible for the training and further education of employees for the state service.[2] The Ministry of Labour takes over the service law.[3] This includes labour and collective bargaining law for employees in the state service, remuneration, personnel administration of all careers and employees, flexitime, holiday and sick leave, working time with or without flexitime in part-time or full-time at the place of work or in home work. The Ministry of Infrastructure provides housing assistance for all state employees.[4] The Ministry of Finance's Pay Office takes care of employees' salary, expenses, travel and relocation costs.[5] The Ministry of Education provides childcare for all employees in the state service.[6]

The Ministry of Health is responsible for the occupational health service.[7] It ensures occupational health management, deals with the treatment, education and prevention of

---

1 Ministry of State Organisation - 2.1.1.1 Personnel board
2 Ministry of Education - 2.1.1.1 Education and training for the state service
3 Ministry of Labour - 4 State enterprises, 13 Labour Directory
4 Ministry of Infrastructure - 2.1.1.1 Housing assistance for state service employees
5 Ministry of Finance - 2.1.1.1 Staff remuneration
6 Ministry of Education - 2.1.1.2 Childcare for state service employees
7 Ministry of Health - 2.1.1.1 Occupational Health Service

occupational accidents, controls and provides occupational health and safety through the health auditors of the Company Auditing Agency.[8]

2.1.2 Organisation

The ministries of media, security, justice, finance, labour, state organisation provide audit services for quality management in the ministry, evaluation of work performance, revenues and expenditures, as well as corruption prevention, sabotage protection and, if necessary, disciplinary matters.[9]

The language service for translating talks or texts is provided by the Ministry of Education.[10] The Ministry of Finance organises the annual budget vote and ensures proper accounting in each ministry.[11] It regulates budget procedures, budget law, staff budgets, departmental budgets, costs and cash management, and assists ministries in budget planning for the budget vote. The Ministry of Labour regulates procurement law and ensures corruption-free state orders and procurement.[12]

The Ministry of Digital Affairs supports the supply of Information Technology.[13] In voting with the Procurement Office of the Ministry of Labour, it takes care of the procurement, provision, maintenance and service of technical devices and software. Much of this is produced in-house to ensure data protection in information and communication technology. Information technology and digitalisation officers audit and advise the ministries. Digital appointment calendar and documentation services are provided as well as a digital policy archive including a library.

---

8 Ministry of Labour - 20.7.2 Health auditor
9 Ministries of Media, Security, Justice, Finance, State Organisation - 2.1.2.1 Audit services
10 Ministry of Education - 2.1.3 Language Service
11 Ministry of Finance - 8 state revenues, 9 state expenditure
12 Ministry of Labour - 6 Procurement Office
13 Ministry of Digital Affairs - 2.1.2.1.1 Supply of Information Technology

2.2 Management Department

The Management Department is the minister's department. With his office team, he provides policy planning and analysis for his ministry and coordinates the relationship between the nation and the municipality through exchanges with his deputies in the municipalities. He initiates cooperation with other ministries or citizens in committees and is supported by the Ministry of State Organisation.

The Ministry of Media Affairs, through its media service, provides press and public relations for the ministry, moderates civil dialogue, trains or provides a spokesperson for the minister, writes speeches and texts on request, and ensures the implementation of conferences and events.[14]

The Ministry of Digital Affairs is responsible for digital management and thus provides departmental management. It automatically produces business statistics, staff surveys and the current state of research through statistics. It automatically forwards proposals to the affected or empowered state employees. In document management, it ensures digitalisation and that ministries share forms with each other.[15]

2.3 European Department

The Ministry of Foreign Affairs ensures the constant transmission of the latest information on current European policy affecting the ministry concerned, applicable European Union law and all European Union funding programmes starting or in progress.[16]

2.4 Department for Barter Economy Zones

The Department of Barter Economy Zone ensures balanced management and structural policies of the different zones, establishes areas and monitors their condition. It provides for administration in cooperation with the offices of the Ministry

---

14 Ministry of Media Affairs - 2.2.1.1 Media Service
15 Ministry of Digital Affairs - 2.1.2.1 Digital Service
16 Ministry of Foreign Affairs - 2.4 European Department

of Barter Economy in the town halls and the residents of the Barter Economy Zone. The Department of Barter Economy Zone is responsible for setting and maintaining standards for immigrants, residents, property and raw materials.

2.5 Department for Economy and Enterprises

The Department for Economy and Enterprises ensures the formulation of draft laws and the execution of laws for immigrants, residents and entrepreneurs in the various comfort levels, settlements and the capital cities of the Barter Economy Zone. This includes, in particular, the requirements vis-à-vis other economic forms, the tax- and fee-funded services of other ministries, laws on legal, natural, labour and health protection, and foreign trade.

2.6 Department for Economic Sectors of the Barter Economy

The Department for Economic Sectors of the Barter Economy develops draft laws together with the affected companies and ensures that the companies implement the laws. Affected companies are always those that have a special role in the economy, such as manufacturing or service companies, private educational institutions, land, real estate or finance economy.

3 Tasks of the Ministry for Barter Economy

The task of the Ministry of Barter Economy is to operate Barter Economy Zones in the specified forest areas, where a near-natural and self-determined way of life is possible. A variety of possible lifestyles is offered through the capital city, settlements and hermits in three comfort levels. Proximity to nature is lived through stone-age or medieval ways of living and working as well as the renunciation of non-rotting objects. Exceptions to the use of modern technology are allowed to protect the environment and regenerative capacity.
Basically, the residents of a Barter Economy Zone administer themselves with direct democratic methods, such as plenary

assemblies, committees, the Settlement Court and the applications on the intranet. They support each other in surviving in nature and share their most useful inventions with each other. The Ministry of Barter Economy supports them in this.

The Ministry of Barter Economy has the task of measuring economic development, preventing shortages and enabling future generations to live in the Barter Economy Zone with sufficient resources. It fulfils this task through strict regulations on environmental sustainability and foreign trade.

With its enterprise policy, the Ministry of Barter Economy fulfils the task of regularisation of payment transactions, default on payment, remuneration and liability in such a way that no money is necessary. With the different economic sectors, the Ministry of Barter Economy enables the provision of housing, investment opportunities, insurance, food, craftspersons' services and trade in goods to the inhabitants.

Since the residents of the Barter Economy Zone do most things on their own, state services are lower. In cooperation with the ministries of security, justice, health, family and education, the basic needs of children, the sick, the injured and the damaged are met. To pay for these services, the Ministry of Barter Economy collects taxes. The taxes are paid in money when money has been earned. Barter taxes can be paid in kind or money.

In certain disaster situations, the Ministry of Barter Economy has the task of transferring the Barter Economy's living and working methods to the whole country and implementing the possible comfort levels in a Planned Economy manner.

4 Economic policy[17]

The Ministry of Barter Economy operates an economic policy that allows the economic form to exist autonomously. The Barter Economy Zones engage in barter trade with each other, which the ministry adapts to the different local conditions and resource deposits in the Barter Economy Zones.

The Ministry of Barter Economy is responsible for all Barter Economy Zones inland and restricts economic freedom

17§210,1,2,5 Principles of the economic order: BV Art. 94, KV Art.50

through its rules. It regulates economic policy issues relating to the labour market and social order. The labour market results from the supply and demand of workers producing goods and services to exchange and thus share labour. The social order is characterised by settlers and hermits living together in three different comfort levels. The Ministry of Barter Economy coordinates and monitors the population and sustainable management of the Barter Economy Zone. This is a competition policy that on the one hand allows competition for the best work performance or the best product and on the other hand prevents ruinous competition that leads to the exploitation of humans and nature.

The regional economic policy is determined by the different local conditions in which the Barter Economy Zones are located and the three comfort levels that divide individual Barter Economy Zones into small regions. The inhabitants live together in a community that is divided into three municipalities. Each municipality shares the same standard of living in its comfort level.

4.1 Barter Economy economic order

The Barter Economy's economic order is shaped by ways of working from the past, when money played no role for humanity. This ensures economic freedom because companies and workers are free to decide whether they want to provide their services in a Stone Age, Medieval or Modern Age way. The welfare and economic security of the population is ensured by making it possible to survive without the latest technology and money in modern times. Should a disaster make the use of modern technology or money impossible, the economy still does not collapse, but can be switched to the Barter Economy way of working.

4.2 Economic development

Regional and overall economic development in all Barter Economy Zones is examined by preparing analyses by the Company Auditing Agency and projections in real laboratories, i.e. in selected companies in the Barter Economy Zone. The key figures of the statistics include the growth of turnover and profits as well as the development of the demographics of employees, pensioners and applicants of the companies. With the help of the key figures, the ministry conducts economic and structural policy research in cooperation with the Company Auditing Agency and the Ministry of Digital Affairs, which provide the necessary data. The aim of the research is to flexibly adjust the amount of raw materials to different population figures while constantly ensuring environmental neutrality and natural renewal capacity, so that future generations can also use the Barter Economy Zone equally well.

4.3 Handbook for survival in nature

The handbook is given to every new resident who does not yet have a current copy. The handbook provides all the information and instructions in words and pictures that are necessary to survive in nature without destroying it in the long term. Edible, healing or useful plants, animals and rocks are shown photographically and, if possible, the processing and use of all end and waste products is described. It is shown how farming, animal husbandry, hunting, house building, water and sewage management can be done in an environmentally friendly way by individuals and groups. The production of simple tools and their use is also shown. The treatment of wounds, diseases that can be caused by animals and plants, the transport of injured people and what to do in the event of fires, floods, storms and thunderstorms form the information for emergencies.

All residents can make requests for changes and suggestions for improvements to the book at the town hall. In the following plenary assembly, the inclusion in the handbook is voted on by all residents. Through constant updating, the book is made available as a ring binder so that subsequent insertion and removal of pages is possible. The handbook is also available as a digital version via the Knowledge Directory.

4.4 Inventions

Residents who invent new things or develop ways to make or process things can report this at the town hall. The Innovation Agency[18] examines the inventions and reports the appropriate industrial property right if the examination is successful. All residents of all Barter Economy Zones are allowed to use the inventions, all other persons of other economic forms have to pay licence fees to the inventors.

As a tribute, the face of the inventor is carved into a living tree. For this purpose, the Ministry of Barter Economy has a small milling machine that can be clipped to a tree and carves the digital image into the bark. The inventor gets to choose the tree, which must be in the Barter Economy Zone where the inventor lives at the time of the invention.

5 Comfort levels

The comfort levels reflect the technical progress in human history. Money and division of labour play different roles in the three comfort levels. The need for a surrounding developed civilisation is greatest in the highest comfort level and least in the lowest. In order to ensure the well-being of the child, children can decide for themselves whether they live in the children's house of the Social Village, in boarding school or with their parents in a comfort level. All children growing up in the Barter Economy Zone receive all vaccinations, except flu shots, upon request.

5.1 Lowest comfort level

Inhabitants live here as they did in the Neolithic period, working as hunters and gatherers, cultivating crops and raising livestock, and producing simple ceramics and metals.

---

18 Ministry of Innovation - 4 Innovation Agency

Mechanical work is mostly done by animals, wind or water. They live in tents, huts or houses made of cloth, animal skin, wood or stone. Urination is done through a rainwater toilet in a septic tank, which must be far enough away from drinking water wells. Cooking and heating is done on a fire stove.

If fuel runs out, residents can stay in emergency shelters in the capital city during winter. If the residents of a Barter Economy Zone ban the burning of wood for heating in a plenary assembly, residents at the lowest comfort level can also use zeolite heaters.

The entry fee includes the flat rate for security and infrastructure as well as training and teaching material. Infrastructure means control of the Barter Economy Zone, emergency shelters, emergency medical care, buildings, lines and roads, and the capital city. Security means police and Company Auditing Agency checks to ensure that laws are being followed and to bring criminals to justice. It also includes the fire brigade and the rescue service.

5.2 Medium comfort level

Residents live here as in the Middle Ages with all the conveniences of modern times and today's technical development, but without any petrochemicals and similar non-decaying products. Mechanical work is done by machines powered by electricity, wind, water or naturally degradable fuels. People live in multi-storey houses made of stone, metal, wood and glass windows. To protect the environment, polluting production activities are carried out in the capital city according to today's environmental protection standards, such as the tanning of leather. Cooking is done on a cooker that can be operated with electricity or biogas. Heating is provided by a biogas plant made from faeces and compost, heat exchangers and zeolite heaters. Light is generated by solar modules, rechargeable batteries and LED lamps. Wastewater from toilets and stables is discharged via a sewer system to a sewage treatment and biogas plant.

The entrance fee includes the flat rate for the lowest comfort level. In addition, there are the costs for the sewage system, sewage treatment plant and biogas plant, as well as handicraft businesses and companies that are available for use free of charge in the capital city.

5.3 Highest comfort level

Here, residents live on the current state of the art, as self-sufficiently as possible in caravans, mobile homes and mobile homes containers on the edge of the Barter Economy Zone on pitches. Each pitch has a connection to the networks for water, sewage, electricity and digital data. Residents can connect to the networks and only have to pay for what they use. Solar panels, wind turbines, heat exchangers, zeolite heaters, sewage gas systems, rain collection systems and water treatment systems can be purchased at the wholesale market to make the living container independent of all networks. Surpluses can be fed into the electricity network if a connection is available. The WLAN signal for the People's Computer is available everywhere inland.

The entrance fee includes all services of the lowest and medium comfort level as well as the construction costs for the pitches. The pitches can only be rented. Rental contracts can be concluded for life and only expire upon the death of the resident. Inheritance is possible, but the currently applicable entrance fee must be paid by the inheritor. Vacancy of more than 8 weeks per year is prohibited. In addition to the entrance fee, equipment such as a self-sufficient living container, with all devices and furnishings, can be booked. The construction is done by experienced craftspersons from the Barter Economy Zone, who can earn money with it or enter into a barter deal with the new owner.

6 Barter Economy Zone

The Ministry of Barter Economy, together with the Ministry of Planned Economy, conducts structural policy inland. Rural regions with high unemployment are preferred locations for Barter Economy Zones. Barter Economy Zones are usually opened in sparsely populated regions, which are often also structurally weak. The capital cities guarantee jobs and security of supply also for residents of surrounding localities.

6.1 Area[19]

There are several Barter Economy Zones throughout the country. Their number and size depends on how many nationals decide to live in the Barter Economy.

The Ministry of Barter Economy expels areas that can be used as Barter Economy Zones. These are state forest areas all over the country and preferably nature parks with large contiguous forest areas that are state-owned and populated with less than 50 inhabitants per square kilometre. In addition, areas are purchased that lie between forest areas and have meadows, streams, rivers, lakes or coastline.

Depending on the size of the area, a maximum number of inhabitants per square kilometre is set so that all available raw materials can be regrown. The Barter Economy areas are marked by border posts that are within sight of each other and to which solar panels and wind turbines are attached. Each area is given a capital city, located at the edge of the area and connected to all networks for infrastructure. Within the area, there are strict environmental regulations determined by the Ministry of Health. Basically, only things that are naturally degradable may be used there, and within a short period of time. The short period should not exceed one human life. Exceptions, such as glass, confirm the rule. The exceptions are again subject to strict rules on disposal and recycling. A residue-free circular economy must be guaranteed. Otherwise, the risk of impairing the protective function of forests is too high.

6.2 Capital city and settlements

Each Barter Economy Zone is structured similarly. There is a capital city with all necessary utilities at a single entry and exit

---

19§193,4 Forest, §191,5 Nature and homeland protection: BV Art. 78, §186,2 Peaceful separation

point. State and private service providers live here and receive income from the Barter Economy Zone as wages and can live without restrictions at the current level of technology. Around the Barter Economy Zone are border fortifications that only get a fence if the inhabitants decide so by direct democracy. Otherwise, the borders are only marked with border posts on which day and night vision cameras are mounted. This is to allow wild animals to cross the borders easily and to prevent illegal immigration or imports. Along the border are buildings and sites for caravans and mobile homes for living at the highest comfort level. Along the border, pipelines for electricity, drinking water and sewage are laid all around the Barter Economy Zone.

There are any number of settlements in the Barter Economy Zone, which can be of different sizes. Hermits live scattered in the Barter Economy Zone and do not have to belong to any settlement. Settlers and hermits live in the middle or lowest comfort level.

6.2.1 Capital city

The capital city provides all state services for education, health, finance and voting. The Ministry of Education runs schools there, which can also be mobile. The Ministry of Health runs a hospital and mobile doctor's surgeries there. The Ministry of Finance runs a branch of the People's Bank[20], which can also be mobile. The Ministry of State Organisation runs the town hall and supports direct democratic voting by residents in the Barter Economy Zone and the capital city. Negotiations and the resulting voting can take place in the town hall square or with a People's Motor Vehicle[21] in the affected settlement and digitally on the intranet.

Modern residential and commercial buildings are permitted in the capital city. This allows service providers and producers to offer their services to residents in the wholesale market.

---

20 Ministry of Finance - 11 People's Bank
21 Ministry of Media - 7.1.1 People's Motor Vehicle

6.2.2 Settlements

Settlements are living and working communities of several inhabitants. In settlements, tree houses, wooden huts or stone houses are built where no one objects. Settlements are characterised by residents living closer together and sharing more work than hermits. Settlements are close to paved roads so that vehicles with mobile schools, doctors' surgeries, People's Bank branches and People's Motor Vehicle can visit the settlements at regular intervals.

6.3 Small Barter Economy Zones

If there are not enough residents in a Barter Economy Zone to cover the costs of all services, the services are replaced. Not all comfort levels can be offered, possibly only the lowest. The nearest Barter Economy Zone can barter services for small Barter Economy Zones. The capital city then becomes the nearest town with a town hall and the hospital is a 20-foot container of an ambulance. The fire brigade must itself be organised as a voluntary fire brigade. To attend school, children must either attend the nearest school or live in the Social Village for 6 months a year and attend school there, or they are home schooled. In the case of home-schooling, school-age children are regularly tested by performance records which they send to the Ministry of Education. The performance records must be submitted unassisted at the intranet café of the nearest town hall or state educational institution.

7 Administration of the Barter Economy Zones[22]

The administration of the Barter Economy Zone is basically carried out centrally. All matters concerning only one Barter Economy Zone are administered municipally by it alone. As an independent municipality, each Barter Economy Zone has the right to administer itself at the municipal level.[23] The self-administration of a Barter Economy Zone can be limited by

22 §130,2,3 Cultural protection areas and economic zones: BV Art.50
23 Ministry of State Organisation - 11.5 Municipal policy, 10 Subsidiarity, 11 Federalism

the constitution and the ministries of labour and health.

The community of the inhabitants of a Barter Economy Zone is organised in the capital city. In the economic sphere, companies of craftspersons and agriculture are run there together. In economic policy areas, plenary assemblies and committees are held in the town hall and town square so that residents can democratically organise their coexistence and negotiate laws in voting with the Ministry of Barter Economy. With other ministries, the Ministry of Barter Economy ensures admission to state services for health, education, child welfare and security.

7.1 Town hall

The town hall is the central administrative office of each Barter Economy Zone. As in any other town hall, all ministries have offices here through which state services are provided.

In the town hall of the capital city of a Barter Economy Zone, there is an office for the Ministry of Barter Economy. It serves as a central point of contact for residents for all information about life in the Barter Economy Zone and the opportunities offered in the capital city to residents and citizens or companies of other economic forms.

In the office of the Ministry for Barter Economy, all motions are submitted when residents of the Barter Economy Zone want to make direct-democratic decisions among themselves. In the course of the next plenary assembly or in a specially convened committee, decisions can be made through discussions and voting. Plenary assemblies are held annually in the town hall square. Committees can be held where the decision fits thematically or on the town hall square.

7.2 Plenary assembly

The date of the annual plenary assembly is determined by the residents themselves at a plenary assembly. As soon as 40% of the residents vote in favour of holding an extraordinary plenary assembly, it is convened. The plenary assemblies focus on the situation of the Barter Economy Zone and its future development. Residents are asked in surveys how they feel, what they lack and what they like. The auditors of the Company Auditing Agency conduct the surveys and check how well the various Barter Economy Zones cover their costs.[24] The focus is on meeting demand, successful goods and services, and how division of labour can lead to greater benefits for all residents. The agenda is set by the Ministry of Barter Economy in accordance with the proposals of the Company Auditing Agency, and residents create their own agenda items through motions. At the beginning of a plenary assembly, a voting takes place to determine when it is the turn of which agenda item.

7.3 Barter Economy Directory

In the Barter Economy directory[25] , all residents have a profile whose contents consist of the Persons Directory and the Labour Directory in order to know the interests and skills of the neighbours. In this way, partners for joint projects can be found quickly. What data the residents share on their profile is up to them.

Each Barter Economy Zone is a group, each settlement a subgroup, consisting of the profiles of all residents. Here, information can be exchanged and voting can be held. Each group receives a start page that is publicly visible and can be freely designed. Each group has a virtual platform to make direct democratic decisions.[26]

The barter shop and the wholesale market have an online shop in the Barter Economy Directory, which can also be reached via the swap shop .[27]

---

24 Ministry of Labour - 20.7.3.7.1 Determining demand
25 Ministry of Digital - 12 Directories
26 Ministry of Digital Affairs - 15.5 Policy Manager
27 Ministry of Digital Affairs - 14.3 Swap shop

7.4 Population

For each Barter Economy Zone, the maximum number of inhabitants is determined by the Ministry of Barter Economy. The decisive limits are set by the inhabitants in voting and by nature through the regenerative capacity of a stable ecosystem. Once the maximum number of inhabitants has been reached, no more inhabitants are allowed to move into this Barter Economy Zone. There are waiting lists for full Barter Economy Zones. As soon as 90% of the capacities of all Barter Economy Zones are exhausted, new areas must be developed to expand existing Barter Economy Zones or new Barter Economy Zones must be created. The same applies in reverse for a decrease in the number of inhabitants.

7.5 Inhabitants

Nationals can move into the Barter Economy Zone. It is possible to move in and out of the Barter Economy Zone several times in a lifetime.

When moving in, knowledge must be proven. To do this, residents must take a test at the capital city school before moving in. The lessons are available digitally in the Knowledge Directory. At the school, there are courses taught by voluntary Barter Economy residents. In the morning, the theory is learned and in the afternoon, the theory is implemented in practice. In the afternoons, the course participants leave the capital city and go to the field to observe how the residents live, build and eat. In the lessons, the careful handling of nature is taught and how to achieve the most yields without damage to nature's ability to regenerate. For this purpose, the handling of the handbook for survival in nature is especially practised.

All belongings are checked to see if they are naturally degradable. All items that are not naturally degradable are either registered or stored, sold or disposed of in the capital city or outside the Barter Economy Zone on your own responsibility. Non-naturally degradable items belonging to guests or tourists must be registered upon entry and removed from the register upon departure. This applies especially to packaging of consumer goods made of non-naturally degradable materials, but also to clothing, for example. Lockers are offered for the temporary storage of items that are not needed in the Barter Economy Zone.

7.5.1 Guests

Guests must be relatives of the residents with whom they stay. Guests must pay for all services and buy additional food at the wholesale market. The host is responsible for his guests. Guests are allowed to bring their belongings into the Barter Economy Zone that they need for the stay.

7.5.2 Tourists

Tourism policy is regulated by the Ministry of Barter Economy to ensure that tourists are a source of income on the one hand, but do not endanger the ecosystem and the security of supply of the inhabitants on the other.

Tourists can stay at the hotel in the capital city and visit the Barter Economy Zone on foot or on horseback. They can stay for up to one month in the comfort level of their election with voluntary residents for rent. Rental contracts for tourists are standardised for each comfort level. The wordings are negotiated between the Ministry of Barter Economy and Barter Economy residents in a direct democratic manner. Tourists have to pay a per diem for their stay in the Barter Economy Zone, the amount of which is determined by the residents directly democratically, but which has to compensate at least all expenses of humans and nature.

7.6 Property

In the Barter Economy area, everything is common property. Only items made by one's own hands belong to the maker(s). Items such as clothes, houses, household goods can be inherited. The common property is used by the inhabitants in a direct democratic way. This is to avoid overconsumption, which would deprive future inhabitants of their livelihoods. Voting is conducted through the town hall in the capital city. The local mayor is responsible for ensuring that his municipality does not live beyond its means.

7.7 Raw materials

Commodities are mineral resources, animals and plants that are located in the area of a Barter Economy Zone. In general, the raw materials are considered common property that is used in the interest of the community and distributed fairly among all current and future inhabitants. This is ensured by direct-democratic committees in the capital city. Raw materials that cannot be extracted locally can be exchanged with other Barter Economy Zones or purchased in other economic forms. Tools are usually needed to extract raw materials. These tools can be bought or lent out in the capital city.

If vital raw materials are no longer available, no one is allowed to move into a Barter Economy Zone. If individual raw materials run out, the Barter Economy Zone municipality must organise itself to go and earn money in other economic forms or sell surplus produce through the barter shop in the capital city or generate revenues through tourism.

7.7.1 Fuels

Wood is a scarce resource in the Barter Economy. It is therefore crucial that only as much of it is consumed as can also grow back. On the one hand, management is based on the maximum number of inhabitants in a Barter Economy Zone. On the other hand, new residents are educated at the beginning in training sessions on how they can heat and build without having to cut down many trees. For example, fuel for the winter can be collected through an annual pruning of trees, shrubs and grasses.

In addition, biogas is produced from the excreta of animals and humans as fuel. Since there are also residential houses in

Barter Economy Zone without a connection to a sewerage system, the construction of a septic tank and the expansion into a biogas plant is taught in the school in the capital city.

The heating systems of the houses work with zeolite. The zeolites are dried in the sun on the roofs and water is poured over them in the houses to heat them.

7.7.2 Water

Admission to irrigation and irrigation water is provided via rainwater catchment systems, channels, streams and lakes. Admission to drinking water is provided via rainwater and wells. The drilling of wells is subject to approval. The prerequisite for this is that sufficient groundwater reserves are available. In principle, every resident is allowed to drill a well, but this is not possible everywhere and is very laborious for one person. Residents can join forces and jointly apply for a well at the town hall. There, it is determined where the next possibility is to drill a well within a radius of the residents' place of residence. Necessary tools can be lent out in the capital city.

Wastewater must be collected and treated in on-site septic tanks, which must be constructed according to certain requirements. If necessary, above-ground or underground channels can also be laid to convey wastewater to a sewage treatment plant. If the sewage treatment plant is not built by the residents themselves, sewage fees must be paid to the Ministry of Infrastructure.

7.7.3 Building material

Besides wood, stones made of hemp and lime or clay can be used as building materials, provided the Barter Economy Zone has these mineral resources. Barter Economy Zones can trade goods in their barter shops in the capital cities, in which individual Barter Economy Zones specialise. For example, there may be a blast furnace in a capital city and a mine in the

Barter Economy Zone.[28] In another Barter Economy Zone there is a quarry, in the capital city a brickyard and a cement plant. This allows scarce goods to be exchanged. The transport costs money and is done through the Social Service of Planned Economy.[29]

7.7.4 Electricity

Electricity is generated by the residents themselves and by the community. Every single resident is entitled to use solar, wind and hydro power to generate electricity or to do work. Residents at the medium and highest comfort levels may purchase solar panels in the capital city to mount on their buildings. The electricity may be used to power sources of light and heat as well as economic and domestic machinery. For residents of the lowest comfort level, there is the possibility to lend out a solar panel for the People's Computer[30] in the town hall, so that these citizens can also participate in direct democracy. The community is supported by electricity generation plants along the boundary posts of a Barter Economy Zone, which is available to all residents and distributed and surpluses sold in direct democratic voting.

8 Switching between economic forms

The Ministry of Barter Economy regulates the transfer and admission of companies from other economic forms into the Barter Economy, as well as the admission of Barter Economy companies into other economic forms. The rules are drawn up in voting with the affected ministries and all residents of the Barter Economy in the plenary assemblies or in committees. The Ministry of Barter Economy's role is to ensure that trade with other economic forms does not limit security of supply and natural renewal capacity. To this end, the Ministry of Barter Economy sets requirements that regularise the import and export of goods and services by Barter Economy residents and companies. The other economic forms can trade with the

28 https://rohstoffportal-sgd.bgr.de/pics/BSK1000_gr.png
29 Ministry of Planned Economy - 9.4.1 Social Service
30 Ministry of Digital Affairs - 13.6 People's Computers

Barter Economy but have no say in how and with whom work is done.

8.1 Entrance and exit of persons and companies

Entrance into the Barter Economy is possible as long as the neighbours within 100 metres do not object to moving in. This applies equally to persons and companies. So if you want to bring your company from another economic form into the Barter Economy, ask the plenary assembly about the need and possible employees. For the audit of changing companies, the Company Auditing Agency carries out special audits.[31] The Ministry of Finance is responsible for changing business tax.[32] There are entry fees when moving in persons and changing companies to the Barter Economy. Depending on which comfort level one books, different fees are due. The fees cover the effort to maintain the infrastructure, which varies depending on the comfort level. The Ministry of Barter Economy calculates the amount of the costs incurred and adds a profit mark-up of 10%. This profit mark-up goes into the savings account of a Barter Economy Zone.

Exit from the Barter Economy is possible at any time. The exit fee results from all outstanding payments and consideration of a resident and his or her company.

8.2 Import and export of goods and services

The import of goods and services is permitted as long as the environmental compatibility of the products is guaranteed. Barter Economy residents must either have enough money to pay for the products or the suppliers accept barter.

Companies in the market economies that want to produce specifically for the Barter Economy can set up in the capital city. Their product range must comply with environmental regulations and use only naturally degradable things. They can charge in-kind or cooperation as the price for their products

---

31 Ministry of Labour - 10.2.2 Changing companies
32 Ministry of Finance - 5.2.7 Business taxes in the economic forms

and negotiate prices with each customer individually.

The export of goods is only permitted if the supply of all inhabitants of the Barter Economy is secured and the regenerative capacity is supported. Services can also be provided by labour outside the Barter Economy. The Ministry of Barter Economy is responsible for calculating the surpluses and communicates the results to the residents of the Barter Economy at the plenary assemblies. There, the residents can determine whether the surpluses actually exist and are reduced or export permits are issued.

9 Enterprise policy[33]

The Ministry of Barter Economy is responsible for the enterprise policy of Barter Economy. It provides for the necessary trade and craft laws to regularise the principles of business management. It ensures economic freedom and freedom of contract and issues necessary exemptions in the interest of the people, the constitution and the environment.

The Ministry of Labour issues the basic regulations for the protection of labour, consumers and nature for entrepreneurs, which are supplemented by the Ministry of Barter Economy. The relationship between employers and employees is defined in barter contracts. Most Barter Economy residents are self-employed and do any work they are willing and able to do. The Ministry of Barter Economy does not allow corporations and splits up companies that exceed a medium size. Joint-stock companies cannot operate or be incorporated in the Barter Economy. Companies operate in the trade, craftsperson and service industries. Residents with special expertise can exercise liberal professions. For each sector there is a chamber in which entrepreneurs, employees and customers can come together to negotiate collective and supply agreements.

Occupational pension schemes are run by each worker him/herself. Companies are not obliged to do so, but can offer it. Occupational pension provision can be invested in kind or in money. In kind are, for example, buildings or machines. Money is, for example, financial services provided by People's

---

33§228,1a,1b Labour: BV Art. 110, §232,1,2b,2c Occupational benefits: BV Art. 113, §216,2 Joint-stock companies

Bank. Both assets can be sold in case of illness or pension. Insurance from other economic forms can be continued through Citizens' Insurance.[34] The requirements of insurance from other economic forms or other ministries apply as insurance law, since the Ministry of Barter Economy does not operate its own insurance.

9.1 Remuneration

Goods and services are remunerated with counter-performance, which the service recipient and the service provider negotiate with each other beforehand. This can be labour, food, clothing, fuel, building materials or other services. The treaties can be made orally or in writing. Oral treaties can be videotaped by the People's Computer by those affected. The treaties should have the performance and the consideration as well as the period in which both performances are to be rendered.

Anyone who cannot provide an agreed consideration must negotiate an additional agreement to the original treaty. If the other party is not satisfied with this, the case can be heard in the Settlement Court.

9.2 Liability

Damage must be made good to the injured party. Damage that all participants contractually accept is excepted from this. Damage is deemed to be damage to another's property or mental and physical integrity as well as the outstanding return of loans. The procedure for compensation corresponds to the remuneration for services. If the question of guilt or the compensation payment is doubted, the Settlement Court can be convened.

---

34 Ministry of Labour - 10.2.4 Citizens' Insurance

9.3 Settlement Court

The Settlement Courts offer free commercial legal protection for the first instance. If further court instances are pursued, the fees set by the Ministry of Justice must be paid.

The Settlement Court only hears compensation claims. It clarifies the question of guilt and the amount and type of compensation payments. The Settlement Court consists of advisors, deciders and jurors. There are at least 10 jurors, as independent as possible, but always an even number, so that the decider can break a deadlock with his vote. Deciders replace judges and must be as independent as possible from both sides. Deciders are also jurors themselves, elected by all jurors to the role of decider. Advisers replace lawyers and are chosen by the plaintiff and defendant themselves. All participants in the settlement court proceedings have equal voting rights when the guilt, amount and type of compensation are voted on. Losers in the proceedings can take the case to the Municipal Court.

The Settlement Court is a panel consisting of residents of the affected Barter Economy Zone. The jurors of the Settlement Court are newly determined by lot for each case. In a plenary assembly, an objection to a decision of the Settlement Court can be raised and another type of appointment to the jurors can be voted on. Settlement Court services are free of charge to plaintiffs and defendants, and jurors serve without pay. Settlement Courts are the first instance to hear economic damages and the failure of agreed services or consideration in Barter Economy transactions.

9.4 Environmental compatibility[35]

Only naturally degradable products may be produced or imported into the Barter Economy. Anything that has rotted in 100 years when exposed to the elements without protection is considered naturally degradable. Many plastics are therefore banned. The Ministry of Innovation audits companies through

---

35§190,1,2,8 Environmental protection: KV Art.31, §191,5 Nature and homeland protection: BV Art. 78

innovation auditors from the Company Auditing Agency to see if and how they are using innovation to implement environmental protection requirements. It is involved in teaching newcomers and collaborates in the formulation of the manual on survival in nature.

Exceptions apply to containers and caravans of the highest comfort level. All non-naturally degradable items must be registered upon import. As soon as these things are disposed of, this must be done via the waste recycling plant in the capital city. There, every registered thing is removed from the register afterwards.

All things traded or consumed in the Barter Economy must be recyclable, even if this requires production steps. If there is no recyclable substitute for essential items, these items may be imported and must be included in the register as hazardous substances.

Disposing of non-naturally degradable items in the forest is punishable by imprisonment.[36]

As consumers, residents and companies must adhere to nature's ability to renew itself and only consume as much as can grow back. Everything that is taken from nature, it must be able to restore within 100 years at the most. The residents of a Barter Economy Zone can set shorter periods so that at least the security of supply of all residents is guaranteed.

9.4.1 Inspection[37]

There are auditors for economy, health and legality in the Company Auditing Agency. They control unannounced and covertly the environmental protection and the requirements for imported goods.[38] On the one hand, environmental protection consists of enforcing the ban on things that are not naturally degradable and strict monitoring of exceptions. On the other hand, environmental protection consists of not burdening nature in the Barter Economy Zone more than it is able to regrow, So-called protection of sustainability. After an

---

36 Ministry of Justice - 8.6.1 Environmental pollution
37 §191.5 Nature and homeland protection: BV Art. 78
38 Ministry of Labour - 20.7.3.7.2 Audit of the environmental impact

audit by the Company Auditing Agency, proposals are made if the same area can be managed more sustainably elsewhere. These solutions will be explored on an ongoing basis and, if successful, will be included in the Success Model Directory[39]. In principle, residents of the Barter Economy share their success models free of charge and publicly in the Success Model Directory for other residents of the Barter Economy. For application in other economic forms, the inventors can demand licence fees.

If the inspection reveals faults in sustainability, these faults must be remedied within 12 months or the number of residents will be reduced. Residents who are forced to move out are determined in a committee. They have the right to relocate to another Barter Economy Zone if they personally cannot be proven to have violated sustainable management. Residents who are forced to move out due to violations are given a last chance in another Barter Economy Zone after 2 years. This means they have to move out of the Barter Economy for 2 years and can then move back in. Those who are then forced to move out again by the community because they have taken resources away from other residents through overconsumption, have committed environmental pollution or violations of sustainable management are not allowed to move into another Barter Economy Zone again. The violation of sustainable management or environmental pollution is resolved by the Municipal Court in the first instance. The limits for overconsumption can be set by residents of a Barter Economy Zone in a plenary assembly and cases of overconsumption can be heard in the Settlement Court.

9.5 Insolvency

Entrepreneurs who become insolvent must negotiate compensation with the affected customers and employees, as in the remuneration procedure. Companies that are established and used by all residents after a majority vote are considered the common property of the residents. These companies cannot become insolvent. If the machines become unusable,

39 Ministry of Labour - 20.9 Success Model Directory

the companies become unable to perform. Worn-out machines are repaired or replaced if a majority of the residents vote in favour and collectively undertake the necessary work.

10 Barter Economy economic sectors

The Barter Economy Zones have various economic sectors that can provide the inhabitants with the goods and services they need to live. This is to meet the special challenge of being able to live in a stone-age, medieval or modern way and still meet all modern technical and health standards.

10.1 Crafts

The crafts are organised in the Barter Economy in a similar way to the early modern period, when there were guilds and manufactories. Every resident is allowed to be a craftsperson. The speciality of the craft enterprises from the Barter Economy is the processing of renewable raw materials into modern products. These products can be used for foreign trade or for the inhabitants of the Barter Economy Zone. Supporting the Barter Economy Zone has priority and natural resources may only be used sustainably. As soon as a resident wants to use the services of a craft enterprise, he must either pay for the service with money, offer his labour, find materials for the service or exchange other products. Craft enterprises do contract work that can be paid for in kind or in money by Barter Economy residents and buyers from other economic forms. Whom a craftsperson serves as a priority is his or her own decision.
Craft workshops are found in the settlements and in the capital city. Manufactories can only be found in the capital city. Craft enterprises working in the settlements may only use tools and materials there that are environmentally neutral. In most cases, processing in the settlements takes place at the place of order or in home work. Between the production of raw materials and the finished product, production steps can be outsourced to the manufactory in order to work with modern machines.

10.1.1 Training

Voluntary do-it-yourselfers are considered apprentices of a guild as soon as they work with a journeyman or master's craftsperson. Journeymen are apprentices who have learnt under a master's craftsperson and become a journeyman after successfully passing an examination organised by the guild. Master's craftspersons are journeymen who have worked in the craft for at least 3 years and have passed a master's examination at a college organised by the responsible educational institution. Part-time study during the 3 years of work experience is possible, as is distance learning. Master's craftspersons and journeymen display their final testimonials in the workshop so that residents know who to contact for questions and orders.

10.1.2 Guilds

The guilds of the time were unifications of master's craftspersons of their trade. The Barter Economy guilds are unifications of master's craftspersons and journeymen. Together they continuously set new standards in quality and working methods. Quality is rated by consumers in the Barter Economy Directory and audited every 2 years by the Company Auditing Agency's technical and health auditors. Crafts can design their own working practices but must report success models to the innovation auditors. Craft businesses can test new standards themselves and propose them to the Company Auditing Agency as part of the questionnaire. The Company Auditing Agency audits innovations immediately for a fee or Tax-funded as part of the next audit.

Guilds regulate the supply of raw materials, employment figures, wages, prices and sales volume for their craft enterprises. Barter Economy residents, on the other hand, can meet a 30% veto quorum to negotiate the rules in a committee. Individual craft enterprises are not forced to adhere to the requirements of a guild as long as they comply with all the requirements of the law.

The traditional guilds are those of shoemakers, weavers,

clothiers, tailors, tanners, saddlers, furriers, fishermen, butchers, millers, bakers, carpenters, painters, bricklayers and roofers. In addition to these 16 guilds, there are 3 guilds for plumbers and heating engineers, electricians and mechanics.

10.1.3 Manufactories

The guilds jointly run the manufactories in the capital city and provide intact or new machines that craft businesses can lend out or use in the manufactory. Guilds of several disciplines share all machines in the workshop wherever this becomes necessary. The factory hall in the capital city is the homeland of all manufactories, which share a common warehouse for raw materials and tools. There are no product warehouses. Products are only stored in the wholesale market until they are sold or exchanged.

Machines are bought as soon as the guild has saved enough money for them. Guilds can demand levies for this purpose from craft enterprises that are members of the guild. If consumers want machines to make products cheaper or better, they can demand the release of the necessary savings from the municipality at the plenary assembly. If a majority of the inhabitants of a Barter Economy Zone vote in favour, the machines are purchased, delivered and set up by the Procurement Office or the responsible guild.

10.1.4 Tools

All tools must be made of biodegradable material. The import of privately owned tools that contain non-biodegradable components is only possible in the workshop. Many tools are rarely needed. Therefore, there is a municipality warehouse in the capital city. Expensive or elaborate tools and machines are usually built or bought jointly by several inhabitants or by guilds in manufactories. These tools and machines can be lent out by other residents and craftsmen. The builders or purchasers of tools and machines determine how high the loan fee should be and at what point all loan fees have paid for the purchase and are then waived. This increasingly increases the stock of tools and machines that residents can lend out free of charge.

Depending on which comfort level residents buy into, they receive a beginner's set of necessary tools and a handbook containing all the necessary information on how to make and use tools.

10.2 Trade

Trade is reserved for two guilds in the Barter Economy. The barterers and the wholesalers. Barterers trade with residents of the Barter Economy and wholesalers. Wholesalers trade with Barter Economy residents, ministries and companies or individuals of other economic forms. Both guilds jointly maintain mail-order trade including logistics in and between the Barter Economy Zones. They can organise transport independently in a merchant train or commission the Social Service.[40]

10.2.1 Barter shop

Barter shops are shops where only residents of the Barter Economy are allowed to trade. In the marketplaces of the settlements and the capital city, residents from one or more Barter Economy Zones exchange their goods and services at stalls. It is possible to digitally enter an offer or demand in the virtual barter shop of the Barter Economy Directory or to pre-order a service. In this way, services can be offered and demanded without the persons and goods having to be on site. Goods and services are described and presented by picture or video. If interested, potential customers can request information or a sample or place orders. The goods and services are then brought to the customer. Surplus goods or services can be offered at the wholesale market.

---

40 Ministry of Planned Economy - 9.4.1 Social Service

10.2.2 Wholesale market

The wholesale market is a large market hall with a heated or refrigerated and illuminated sales area as well as parking spaces and loading ramps. Here, goods and services can be offered for sale or exchange. All nationals and companies are entitled to sell. All humans residing inland are entitled to buy or barter. Traders who are Barter Economy residents do not have to pay a stall fee. For all other traders, a stall fee applies depending on the square footage used. Perishable goods will be given away in the barter shop from the expiry date of the best-before date. A location on the outside of the capital city with good transport links facilitates trade with the area outside the Barter Economy Zone. Traders belonging to the Barter Economy must prove that their export of products does not prevent them from growing the necessary raw materials quickly enough.

In a separate area, only goods and services may be offered that are naturally degradable and can therefore be imported into the Barter Economy Zone. For example, tools may only be made of wood and metal, or paint may only be made of biodegradable paint.

The assortment includes all goods and services that suppliers want to offer. It ranges from food to building materials and tools to clothing and machinery. Not everything is always in stock at the wholesale market. Large machinery, such as a covered wagon for 4 horses, can be ordered via a catalogue.

Non-Barter Economy traders wishing to trade in this area must register their goods and services in advance with the wholesale market management and have them audited by the Company Auditing Agency's auditors.[41] Any packaging materials must be compostable. Barter Economy residents may only import goods and services into the Barter Economy Zone from this area of the wholesale market.

---

41 Ministry of Labour - 20.7.3.7.3 Audit of imports and exports

10.2.3 Mail order

The entire assortment of the wholesale market and the barter shops can be viewed and ordered in the Barter Economy Directory. Since every citizen has admission to a People's Computer at any time, all necessary digital work steps can be taken with it.

The payment method must be specified when payment is made. If goods or services are specified for exchange as payment, the payment is not completed until the buyer and seller mark the payment as completed. In an informative description and representation, the consideration must be described by the buyer in the same way as the seller has described his performance.

The logistics centre is located at the wholesale market and is responsible for broadcasts from postcards to beef cattle. Orders can then be picked up or delivered either at the wholesale market or a specified barter shop. Shipments are delivered by the shipping department using livestock or vehicles to the address or coordinates where the People's Computer is located or specified by the buyer. Shipping charges are paid by the buyers.

11 Real estate sector[42]

The Ministry of Barter Economy, in voting with the Ministry of Infrastructure, expels Barter Economy Zones within the country and issues regulations so that land is developed for housing in Barter Economy Zones and building land is released. Land cannot belong to any resident, it belongs to the people and is common property. Real estate, on the other hand, can belong to Barter Economy residents, which the ministry regulates in the Home Ownership Law. They build their houses according to the regulations of the Ministry of Infrastructure, and for the purpose of construction rationalisation, they are inspected by technical auditors of the Company Auditing Agency[43] for their structural stability. In case of deficiencies, the residents have to undertake structural

---

42§226.3 Housing and home ownership promotion: BV Art. 108
43 Ministry of Labour - 20.7.4 Technical auditor

measures for which they are advised by the technical auditors. Once the deficiencies are rectified, it has to be reported at the office of the Ministry of Infrastructure in the town hall. Thereafter, an unannounced inspection takes place.

11.1 Moving in

New residents must ask their potential neighbours if they can live next to them. From a radius of 100 metres, no neighbour needs to be asked. Residents without neighbours are considered hermits who support themselves as much as possible. In the Barter Economy Zone town hall, you can search for available housing locations in the Real Estate Directory on the intranet café. Every day there is new map material for the Barter Economy Zone, delivered daily by satellite. This allows new settlers to see where there is still plenty of space or where there are already settlements that have expelled building plots or where houses, flats or rooms are being rented or sold. Newcomers can move in or build a dwelling there.

To help newcomers find their location, they are allowed to take a navigation device with the point of their residence stored in it or lend it out at the local intranet café and return it within a week.

Newcomers have a trial period of no more than 2 months until the municipality of a settlement votes on the final acceptance of a newcomer. If the newcomer has already built a house by then, the municipality must compensate him for this. Municipalities may decide that newcomers are not allowed to build a house during the probationary period.

11.2 Home buyers and sellers

Buyers of a house can buy or exchange an existing house. Sellers can be residents who are moving out or a settlement municipality. Those moving out of a house can bequeath it, sell it through the Real Estate Directory or give it to the settlement municipality. Houses may be empty for a maximum of 8 weeks per year when residents travel. If houses are sold or exchanged, the seller's move-out date determines the buyer's move-in date. Vacancy is only permitted for a maximum of 8 weeks.

If houses are not occupied again by other residents within 8 weeks after moving out, the house must be donated to the settlement community. The profits that arise when donated houses are sold by the settlement community go into an account of the settlement at the People's Bank. The amount of money may only be invested in the Barter Economy Zone and may not be paid out to the residents of the settlement.

11.3 Tenant and landlord[44]

The ministry regulates the rights and obligations for tenants and landlords in the tenancy law. Landlords can be all residents who have sufficient space, equipment and food in their house to accommodate one or more other residents. Tenants can be all residents who do not wish to live in a house they have built or bought. Tenant and landlord negotiate in the tenancy agreement what the tenant must provide in return to be allowed to live in the landlord's house. The tenancy agreement must be published on the property's profile in the Real Estate Directory. Landlords must first ask the settlement community if the tenant is allowed to move in. If food might become scarce, the influx may be prohibited.

12 Finance economy

The Barter Economy does not operate its own finance economy. Only other ministries provide finance economy services. The Ministry of Finance is responsible for currency and banking, the Ministries of Labour, Health, Justice and Economic Affairs for insurance.

---

44 §227 Rental business: BV Art. 109

12.1 Currency[45]

The Barter Economy money market consists of goods and services. Currencies have the advantage of informing users as fully as possible about their value and condition. In return, barterers must answer truthfully all questions concerning the good or service to be exchanged. To confirm the truth of the information, barterers give their word of honour. Barter is legally equivalent to purchase. Those who deceive in barter face similar sentences as money counterfeiters.

The Barter Economy credit market consists of promises to deliver goods and services in the future. Lenders perform immediately and borrowers perform in return within a fixed period of time. The consideration is naturally higher to compensate for the time and risk of default. Money lending is prohibited in the Barter Economy and is only possible in disaster situations.

12.2 Banks[46]

The financial market of the Barter Economy is limited to the financial services of the People's Bank. The People's Bank is responsible for switching capital between the other economic forms and the Barter Economy. On a goods account, residents can deposit their goods as an image file. To do this, People's Bank staff must inspect and photograph all goods themselves. If the goods cannot be brought to the People's Bank branch, the bank employees come to the customers in the Barter Economy Zone. If the residents exchange one of these goods, they have to confirm the transaction with their People's Computer.

All existing bank accounts outside the People's Bank must be closed when moving in to the Barter Economy and any assets must be transferred to the account at the People's Bank. Residents operating companies in other economic forms must also maintain the company account with the People's Bank. Money can be invested with the People's Bank in a variety of

45 §219.3a Central Bank and Currency Policy
46 §217,1,2 Banks and insurance companies: BV Art.98, §218,5,6 State Bank, §219,5 Central Bank and Currency Policy

ways to offset inflation and generate profits. Capital gains are taxed at 10% business tax.

12.3 Insurances[47]

Citizens' Insurance[48] enables the exchange of capital paid into insurance policies. Provided there are sufficient assets or sufficient money is earned, all insurance policies taken out by the resident can continue. Residents who are retired receive pension payments through Citizens' Insurance into their People's Bank account.

13 Agriculture[49]

Barter Economy agriculture is based on hunting, gathering, farming and animal husbandry. It is designed to support all inhabitants of a Barter Economy Zone with food. In order to ensure that the food supply for humans and animals is as abundant as possible, fields and forests are cultivated according to the permaculture model. Arable farming and small-scale livestock breeding are practised in the fields, and edible forest plants are grown in the undergrowth in the forests. Large livestock live in the wild and are hunted. The field and forest paths can also be visited by tourists, whereby forests fulfil their welfare function. Forests fulfil the protective function of providing a temperate climate and the utilitarian function of supplying food and building material.

The agriculture and forestry sectors work with artisan enterprises to produce food, such as food, hygiene products, clothing and building materials. The Ministry of Barter Economy supports farmers by giving advice on where which crop grows best, how many animals live there and by distributing seeds from seed banks run jointly with the Ministry of Planned Economy.[50]

---

47 §217.3 Banks and insurance companies: BV Art.98, §219.5 Central Bank and currency policy
48 Ministry of Labour - 10.2.4 Citizens' Insurance
49 §220,1a,1c,1f,2 Agriculture: BV Art. 104, KV Art.51
50 Ministry of Planned Economy - 14.5.3.1 Seed Banks

13.1 Forestry

Because Barter Economy Zones are located in state forest areas, forestry is carried out there by a state enterprise. The forestry work is carried out according to public orders by residents who have to provide their labour in order to pay their tax debt in kind. The Central Participation Unit in the Ministry of Barter Economy organises the award of public orders and is supervised by the Procurement Review Board at the Company Auditing Agency's tax auditors.[51]

13.2 Hunting rights

All residents are allowed to hunt and fish. Stock protection applies, so that only as many animals are shot as necessary to keep the stock level. As the population increases, the stock should also grow and be kept at the new higher level. Once a week, a drone with an infrared camera flies over the area to record the wildlife population. The data from the overflight is also used to record the number of inhabitants. Once a year, a sonar buoy is towed through streams, rivers and lakes to record the fish population.
It is not allowed to hunt with firearms. Pistols, rifles or other firearms with propellants and projectiles are prohibited. Hunting is done with weapons such as arrows, spears, networks, traps or fishing rods. Biodegradability is also a basic condition for the use of all hunting tools.

14 Foreign trade[52]

The Ministry of Barter Economy issues foreign trade legislation that regulates the admission of foreign companies and trade in foreign goods and services. International economic and monetary issues are delegated to the ministries of market economy. Export to foreign countries is only possible through companies registered in the Free Market Economy or Social Market Economy. The Barter Economy only barters directly with barter economies of other countries that are in

---

51 Ministry of Labour - 20.7.1.3 Procurement Review Board
52 §225,1,3 Foreign trade policy: BV Art. 101

an International Union with the inland. These agreements between ministries of Barter Economy of different countries, are jointly voted with the Ministries of Foreign Affairs and Labour and the people.

15 Tax policy

The Ministry of Barter Economy's fiscal policy relies on permanent and fluctuating revenue sources. The tax policy also allows in-kind tax contributions in the Barter Economy.
Permanent sources of revenue, which depend on the number of inhabitants, are value added taxes and business taxes. Sellers have to pay business taxes, buyers value added taxes. Residents who do not earn money through their work but barter must hand in their taxes in kind at the Ministry of Finance office in the town hall for this barter. The in-kind goods and services are issued to state workers who work in the capital city of a Barter Economy Zone or sold through the wholesale market to earn money. Residents who earn capital gains through their assets must pay the corporate tax rate to the Ministry of Finance for them. The same applies to Barter Economy companies that earn money through their services. When goods and services are exported to other economic forms or imported into the Barter Economy, the Ministry of Barter Economy may impose tariffs on them. The level of tariffs may vary in different Barter Economy Zones and must be voted on with all affected residents.
Fluctuating sources of income are the fees for the entrance for people moving in and for tourists. The wholesale market in the capital city generates profits through its fees for stalls, digital sales and logistics. The fluctuating sources of revenue are sources of money to pay for goods and services from other economic forms or ministries.
Permanent revenue sources guarantee state services. The fluctuating sources of revenue depend on the voting behaviour of the residents. They vote on how high the fees are for influx and for tourists. Therefore, the fluctuating revenues are paid into the savings balance of each settlement. This can be used to buy new machines, rare raw materials or skilled workers that benefit the general welfare of the inhabitants.

15.1 Value added taxes[53]

Value added taxes are given in kind to keep state employees fed and clothed and buildings equipped and intact. Food and labour are demanded from Barter Economy Zone residents every week, as tithing once was[54] .

For in-kind goods, a list is made for goods that residents produce and state employees need. Food varies seasonally and depends on the crop yield. All other goods are produced at the request of state employees. State employees enter their requests in a list via the Barter Economy Directory and are automatically shown when the maximum amount of goods and working hours of the residents have been reached. Each resident must perform 4 hours of work per week to produce goods or provide services that are on the list. The duty roster is created directly by the residents in the Barter Economy Directory.

The Ministry of Barter Economy determines the content of the list in the Barter Economy Directory at the annual plenary assembly with residents and state employees. For this, a digital estimate is made of how much a state employee needs per day to live and how much is produced by all residents. The type and amount of goods to be supplied should be set in such a way that supply is supported at all times.

Of the food yields, 10% must be delivered to the wholesale market every week. State employees can pick up the food there. Goods that have not been picked up after 2 days are sold. The proceeds go to the wholesale market.

15.2 Business taxes[55]

Companies operated by residents of the Barter Economy Zone are liable for tax, but can pay in kind. In-kind payments consist of goods and services that are used to maintain the infrastructure and natural resources in the Barter Economy Zone. What and how much of it is necessary is determined by the deputy minister for Barter Economy in voting with the

53§151,1,2 Value added tax: BV Art.130
54https://de.wikipedia.org/wiki/Zehnt
55§150,1,3a,4 Business taxes

residents of his or her Barter Economy Zone. All goods and services that are sold rather than traded with Barter Economy residents are taxable. Companies that thus trade with the market economy must pay tax on the resulting profits at the business tax rate of 10%.

15.3 Profit taxes

Residents who own companies in the Social Market Economy or the Free Market Economy can continue to run them. However, they must transfer all bank accounts of the companies to the People's Bank. The business taxes and requirements of the economic forms remain. In addition, the receipt of profits from the company account to the resident's private People's Bank account must be taxed at 10%.

15.4 Taxes on investment income

Residents who have money in their People's Bank account and generate interest income above the inflation rate of the national currency have to pay 10% tax on it. People living in the Barter Economy are only allowed to have one account with the People's Bank, no other accounts with other banks.

16 State services

In the Barter Economy, state services such as security, law enforcement, education, health, election and decision-making are provided. Children do not have to pay for these services. Age of majority pay taxes and have to pay extra for additional services. The election and decision-making procedures are organised by the ministries of state organisation, digital, media and Barter Economy. The People's Computers and the Intranet Café including the voting booth are the means of co-decision as usual.

16.1 Security

The Ministry of Security also provides security in the Barter Economy Zone. The equipment remains largely the same, as the security forces are not subject to the environmental protection requirements imposed by the Ministry of Barter Economy. Only the means of transport are different. The police patrols are on horseback. Police and emergency medical services receive support from the security forces' helicopter squadrons. Vehicles for fire brigades, police and emergency doctors can be equipped with tyres or chains. For this purpose, standardised 20-foot containers with equipment are placed on different floor groups. Emergency ambulances are operated by the Ministry of Security and equipped with devices, materials, physicians and paramedics by the hospital.

Each Barter Economy Zone receives a modified version of the armoured recovery vehicle[56] , which can be used as a construction vehicle and fire-fighting vehicle. In contrast to the military model, it has a longer crane that can also be used as a ladder and has a fire-fighting water pipe. A fire cannon is attached to the end of the fire water pipe.[57] In addition, a 20-foot container can be transported and dropped off at the operation site.

People's Computers serve as emergency call devices and emergency call devices can be lent out at the Ministry of Security office in the town hall. These emergency call devices are supported by electricity via a battery and a hand crank and enable an automatic emergency call in which the position coordinates and personal health data are transmitted. It is also possible to establish a radio connection to the capital city via WLAN or satellite.

In the event of a large fire, the supply of fire-fighting water is ensured via a pipeline. This pipeline is housed in a separate 20-foot container. It is long enough to be laid from the centre of the Barter Economy Zone to the border. To be able to lay the pipeline quickly, the emergency vehicle drives along the border road and unloads the container at the appropriate place. From there, drones fly the empty hose to the operation

56https://de.wikipedia.org/wiki/Bergepanzer_B%C3%BCffel
57Ministry of Security - 5.3 Fire Brigade

site and then lower the line to the ground. Now water is pumped to the operation site from a hydrant at the border of the Barter Economy Zone. The power line supports the pump for the fire water line.

16.2 Medical care

Physicians who are residents of Barter Economy support the other residents and receive services in return. They mainly use naturopathy treatment methods wherever possible. Medicinal plants and naturopathy are used in the hospital and taught in courses. The latest research results and application methods come from the research laboratories of Planned Economy.

The physicians collect the natural resources for the natural therapies together with recovering patients in the Barter Economy Zone. The production and procurement of medical devices or medicines as well as the care of sick patients are part of the consideration for treatments. If devices or medicines are needed that the physician has to buy, the physician can demand a sum of money to cover the expenses.

If an illness is serious or an emergency, residents can go to hospital. Anyone who does not want to go to hospital under any circumstances must indicate this in a living will when moving in at the Ministry of Health town hall office. Those who do not want to go to hospital for an illness can tell the physician and not call the emergency ambulance in an emergency.

The hospital in the capital city is run by the Ministry of Health and has modern equipment. It consists of operating theatres, rooms with as many beds as possible, an emergency room and medical practices with specialists. The treatments in the hospital are chargeable. After recovery, patients have to go and earn money in a company in the capital city, the wholesale market or, if necessary, in one of the market economies until they have paid back the amount. In the meantime, the Ministry of Barter Economy takes out an interest-free loan from the People's Bank and transfers the amount due to the Ministry of Health. If residents are insured with a health insurance company that covers all costs, the repayment obligation does not apply. If the health insurance does not cover all costs, the repayment obligation exists for the outstanding amounts. If patients die, relatives can be held liable for the costs. Foreseeable fatal diseases and injuries are not treated, only pain is relieved.

16.3 Child welfare[58]

The municipality organises childcare and must send childcare workers who do so regularly to the capital city for further training. Parents have the obligation to have their children regularly examined by the paediatrician. The paediatrician visits each child and carries out all preventive medical check-ups and, if necessary, vaccinations. He or she may order the child to come to his or her practice in the hospital at certain appointments if modern or sterile equipment is necessary. For children, all examinations and treatments, of whatever kind, are free of charge. Children are insured through the child benefit in the General Health Insurance .[59]

The paediatrician's appointments take place every 3 months from the time the pregnancy is established until the child's third birthday, every 6 months from the third to the sixth birthday and every 12 months from the sixth birthday until the age of majority. The paediatrician checks at all appointments whether there is a risk to the child's well-being.

Parental protection as part of the best interests of the child consists of the parents' right to care for their child during the first two years of life. If they exercise this right, they can move into a Social Village. All their belongings, including housing, can be stored or lent out to the municipality for this period. The condition of borrowed items must be as good or better than before when they are returned.

---

58 §234,3,4 Children's rights, child benefit and parental protection
59 Ministry of Health - 5.12.2 General Health Insurance

16.4 Education[60]

The Barter Economy's education policy is adapted to life circumstances. The teaching times can be freely chosen, sometimes part-time, sometimes full-time, sometimes from home. The teaching locations can be offered in settlements if there is a sufficient number of students. In distance learning, any educational qualification can also be obtained via the People's Computer and the Knowledge Directory. Educational institutions pay special attention to adapting the vocational education and training of skilled workers to the needs of the companies. This concerns in particular the employment of teachers who can train the old crafts of the guilds and adapt new craftspersons to the conditions in the three comfort levels. The Ministry of Education interviews the companies in the questionnaires during the Company Auditing Agency audit.

The continuing education measures required for admission to the Barter Economy Zone are offered free of charge at educational institutions in the capital city.

All educational institutions are located in the capital city. Provided there are enough teachers who are themselves residents in the Barter Economy Zone, these teachers may open a primary school in the Barter Economy Zone. The curriculum there is the same as in all domestic primary schools. The comprehensive school in the capital city offers weekday half-day schooling and a shortened boarding school. In this type of boarding school, students spend half a year in the capital city and the other half in the Barter Economy Zone with their families. For the time in the Barter Economy Zone, the pupils receive work assignments. Preferably, the boarding school periods are in the winter months.

16.4.1 School route

Learners can lend out bicycles from the educational institution to travel to and from school. The bicycles are all-terrain and have dynamo-powered lights. School buses are only provided

---

60§181.3 Vocational education and training, §182.1 Continuing education and training: BV Art. 64a

in exceptional cases when the nearest educational institution is at least 10 kilometres away. If an educational institution in the surrounding area is closer than the one in the capital city, these educational institutions can also be attended.

16.4.2 Compulsory education[61]

Children living in the Barter Economy Zone also have compulsory schooling from the age of 6 to 18. Parents and children can choose to attend school or Home-schooling. Home-schooling is only possible if the children say at school, without their parents, that they also want home-schooling. The children are told that they are free to decide whether they want to be taught at home or at school at any time up to the end of their compulsory education. If the children make a decision, they can only change their mind after one year, but at least until the end of the current school year.

16.4.3 Home-schooling

Parents are allowed to teach their children themselves if they take tests for each class level and course before teaching their child. Therefore, parents must go to school once a year to take the test for the respective central performance record whose content they want to teach. If they do not pass this test, they must be present during a teacher's lesson preparation and teach a lesson once themselves at school under the supervision of the teacher. Parents can also hire persons for Home-schooling. These private teachers must also pass the above tests.

Children must attend school once a year for one week and pass the central performance records in each subject. Children who score lower than grade 4 in a performance record must attend school lessons in that subject until they achieve grade 2 in the subject.

Children who have a grade point average above 3 on their testimonial must attend school in all subjects until the grade point average falls to or below 2.5.

---

61 §177.8 School system

17 Disaster management[62]

Barter Economy is particularly relevant to disaster management when there is a disaster that destroys or severely disrupts the electricity network or data processing equipment. Because the way of life in the Barter Economy, at least in the lowest and medium comfort levels, is able to support humans without electricity and digital data, this way of life is transferred to all citizens in the event of a disaster. Residents of the two low comfort levels will then be spread across the country to guide citizens on how to live without electricity and digitalisation. All citizens will be trained to become craftspersons of the guilds and farmers in abbreviated training courses. Exactly who has what task will be determined in the emergency plan once the emergency has been rehearsed.[63] The rehearsal is repeated every 10 years. Persons who have now come of age must decide on their role in disaster management and enter their decision in the emergency list.

Even though droughts, floods and forest fires are made unlikely by permaculture, they cannot be completely ruled out. In this case, voluntary residents are evacuated by the disaster management. Those who do not wish to do so must report it via their People's Computer. The disaster management staff will then not seek out that person. Residents are first taken to surrounding Social Villages. Afterwards, all able-bodied residents go back to the disaster area and live in a mobile Social Village until the reconstruction is completed.

18 Switching to the new system

The domestic state forest undergoes territorial reform. The state forest of the regions becomes the property of the nation. Forests are exchanged to create large contiguous areas in sparsely populated areas. Swapping forests means selling forest land in exchange for buying the same or higher number of square metres of land area to connect existing state forests. Gradually, more state forests are released for settlement. Municipal state forests can accommodate individual forest dwellers who are responsible for forest work in return.

62§211,1,4 National supply: BV Art. 102
63Ministry of Security - 5.7.3 Emergency plan

Cities become capital cities on the edge of an area designated as a Barter Economy Zone and are designated as such by majority vote of all affected citizens of the city.

18.1 Conversion of the old ministries

The following is a list of all the departments and units that are transferring to the Ministry of Barter Economy. If only the department or sub-department is mentioned, all its units will be transferred. If individual units are named, only those units are transferred. All departments and units not named are dropped. Existing staff adapt their tasks to the new requirements. The corresponding names of the units can usually be found as keywords in the running text.

18.1.1 Federal Ministry for Economic Affairs and Energy[64]

I Economic policy
Fundamental issues of economic policy, economic policy issues of the labour market and social order, fiscal policy, economic policy coordination, tax policy, Competition and structural policy, consumer policy, fundamental competition policy issues of digitalisation, regional economic policy, money, credit and financial markets, real estate sector, Macroeconomic development, analyses and projections, economic policy analysis, real laboratories, observation, analysis and projection of macroeconomic development, growth, demography, statistics, economic and structural policy research

VII SME policy
Service industry, trade and advertising industry, tourism policy Crafts, Chambers of Commerce and Industry, Promotion of crafts and trades, Liberal professions, Trade law, Education policy, Vocational education and training, Skilled workers, Qualification of volunteers, Digital education

---

64https://www.bmwi.de/Redaktion/DE/Downloads/M-O/organisationsplan-bmwi.pdf?__blob=publicationFile Version: 15.02.201

18.1.2 Federal Ministry of Justice and Consumer Protection[65]

III Trade and Commercial Law
Corporate constitution, Foreign trade law, trade and craft law,
insurance law, fee law in the field of industrial property protection

18.1.3 Bavarian State Ministry of Justice[66]

D Civil law and consumer law
Tenancy law and condominium law

65   https://www.bmjv.de/SharedDocs/Downloads/DE/
Ministerium/Organisationsplan/Organisationsplan_DE.pdf;jsess
ionid=A807B5B1F5EFC74825E8B2A6508405BE.2_cid297?__
blob=publicationFile&v=131 Viewed on: 14/05/2019
66https://www.justiz.bayern.de/media/pdf/orgplan/
organigramm__18042019.pdf Status: 18.04.2019

Contact form

Dear reader
If you would like to make what you have read come true, in whole or in part, together with other like-minded people, I offer you several possibilities with this contact form. Fill it out, tear out the page and send it by post to:
Andreas Seidl, P.O. Box 1206, 63488 Seligenstadt / Germany

Or send the details to:
Phone: 0049 1522 818 2243 (whatsapp, telegram, signal)
Email: andreas.seidl2022@web.de

Please mark with a cross:
O   I want to found a dynamic People's Party.
O   I want to donate money for implementation.
O   I want contacts with like-minded people in my area.

Forename: _____

Surname: _____

Please fill in only the contact option through which a reply should be made.

Street, house no.:   _____

Postcode, city, country: _____

Phone: _____

Email address: _____